Immanuel Haller

# Israel and the Church

GRIN Verlag

**Bibliografische Information der Deutschen Nationalbibliothek:**

Die Deutsche Bibliothek verzeichnet diese Publikation in der Deutschen National-
bibliografie; detaillierte bibliografische Daten sind im Internet über http://dnb.d-
nb.de/ abrufbar.

**Imprint:**

Copyright © 2007 GRIN Verlag GmbH
Druck und Bindung: Books on Demand GmbH, Norderstedt Germany
ISBN: 978-3-656-22376-4

**This book at GRIN:**

http://www.grin.com/en/e-book/196319/israel-and-the-church

**GRIN - Your knowledge has value**

Der GRIN Verlag publiziert seit 1998 wissenschaftliche Arbeiten von Studenten, Hochschullehrern und anderen Akademikern als eBook und gedrucktes Buch. Die Verlagswebsite www.grin.com ist die ideale Plattform zur Veröffentlichung von Hausarbeiten, Abschlussarbeiten, wissenschaftlichen Aufsätzen, Dissertationen und Fachbüchern.

**Visit us on the internet:**

http://www.grin.com/

http://www.facebook.com/grincom

http://www.twitter.com/grin_com

# CONTINENTAL THEOLOGICAL SEMINARY

## CHURCH AND ISRAEL

An essay prepared

For the course:
Ecclesiology (TH 301)

by
Immanuel Haller

Brussels, Belgium
Semester 1, December 2007

# TABLE OF CONTENTS

# INTRODUCTION

The relationship of Israel to the New Testament Church has always been a great theological battleground, and a challenging topic among Christians since the early days of the church. On the one hand some reformed Theologians see literal Israel as virtually swallowed up or displaced by the church or spiritual Israel.[1] On the other hand, dispensationalists regard Israel and the Church as two eternally separate entities with which God deals in different ways.[2] This papers aim is to present an ecclesiological argument regarding the topic of the "Church and Israel." The eschatological significance of Israel is not taken into consideration.

Firstly, we will see what the Olive Tree in Romans 11 could mean. Secondly, we will see the covenant of God with mankind. Thirdly, we will discover the similarity, and fourthly the difference between Israel and the Church.

---

[1] Louis Berkhof, *Systematic Theology* (Grand Rapids: Eerdmans, 1953), 570.
[2] Lewis Sperry Chafer, *Systematic Theology*, vol. 4 (Dallas: Dallas Seminary, 1948), 29.

# ISRAEL AND THE CHURCH

## The Olive Tree in Romans 11

The enigma of the Olive Tree

The Olive Tree in Romans 11 has been an enigma to many Bible interpreters throughout the centuries of the Church age.[3] Most amillennial commentaries have jumped to the conclusion that the Olive Tree is the Church, beginning in Old Testament times and continuing on to the present in its current form. According to this view the Church becomes the new improved Israel, and the Jewish people are relegated to the dustbin of history as an irrelevant part of God's plan, sort of like an appendix – a vestigial organ.[4] With this kind of thinking the replacement theology was born and continues as the view of the vast majority of church scholars.

At the other extreme, some more recent interpreters have suggested that the Olive Tree is Israel, the Jewish people, and the Gentile believers, through their being grafted in, have become Israelites, now have a "Jewish heart," and have considered themselves as Jews.[5]

The Olive Tree is not the church

According to the writers understanding, the Olive Tree is the not the Church. Some people are born naturally into the Olive Tree, but no one is born physically into the Church, the Body of Christ.[6] There is only one way to enter into the body of Christ. It is by being born again by personal faith in the Lord Jesus (John 3:16). Furthermore, it is clear from the New

---

[3] Thomas S. McCall, "What is the Olive Free?" in *Levit Letter*, March 2001, http://www.levitt.com/essays/olivetree-church.html  (24 November 2007).

[4] Ibid., 2.

[5] Ibid.

Testament that the Church began at Pentecost. The Olive Tree, which began with Abraham, Isaac and Jacob cannot be identical to the Church.

## The Olive Tree is not Israel

Also, the Olive Tree cannot be Israel. Some natural branches are broken off the Olive Tree, representing the Jews who do not believe in Jesus the Messiah, even though they are physically still alive. They are physically alive but are spiritually dead, broken off branches.[7] However, no one can be broken off from Israel, as long as he is physically alive. Once a person is born into the covenant nation of Israel, he remains with in it until physically dead.[8]

## The meaning of the Olive Tree

With regard to Ephesians 3:15 the writer agrees with the suggestion of Thomas S. McCall that the Olive Tree represents one people of God, the spiritual Commonwealth of Israel.[9] It is spiritual, because only righteous, born-again, blood-bought believers are in the Olive Tree, whether Jews or Gentiles. It pertains to Israel, because the roots are the fathers of Israel – Abraham, Isaac and Jacob – and the natural branches are Messianic Jews, who remain in the Olive Tree by virtue of their faith in Yeshua, the Christ.[10]

---

[6] Ibid.
[7] Ibid.
[8] Ibid.
[9] Ibid.
[10] Ibid., 3.

## God's covenant with mankind

### Abraham

The covenant began with God's creation of a paradise in the garden (Genesis 2). This was the place were people could receive all of God's blessings, and commune in fellowship with Him. Later on, after the tragic fall of man, God made a covenant with Abraham. Genesis 15:5 tells us: "Abraham believed in the Lord, and He accounted it to him for righteousness." On this basis we read later in Genesis 17:7, that God made an everlasting covenant with him and his desendants through the sign of circumcision for all male people.

### God's people by faith

While the sign of the covenant had to be applied indiviudually to each person we see later on, the Ark of the Covenant served as an objective sign for the whole group of people. On the basis "and he believed God" Abraham became the leader of all pilgrims who seek a city whose builder and maker is God.[11] Throughout God's Word, Abraham is remembered as the father of Israel as well as the father of a new spiritual race.[12] With regard to Hebrews 11 we see in fact, that already Abel, Enoch, Noah and after him Isaac, Jacob, Joseph, Moses, the harlot Rahab, Gideon, Samuel and David went on this race which we see expressed by Abraham "and he believed in the Lord."

---

[11] Hebrews 11:10

[12] The New Thompson Study Bible, (Wollerau, CH: La Buona Novella Inc. Bible Publishing House, 2006), 17.

## God's identification with His people

In spite of human weaknesses and failures, God repeatedly identified himself with His people and expressed His love to those who "belived in the Lord." He even called His people "the apple of His eye," (Deuteronomy 32:10). On the other hand His people expressed their love in Exodus 15:13 by saying "In your unfailing love you will lead the people you have redeemed. In your strengh you will guide them to your holy dwelling…" Throughout the whole Bible we see the thought that God wanted to have His people without reservation and without dividing their loyalty.

## God's people in the New Testament

The pattern of Genesis 15:5 "Abraham *believed in the Lord*, and He accounted it to him for righteousness." can be seen not only in the Old Testament but also throughout the whole New Testament. The scripture in John 3:16 "That *whoever believes in* Him (*The Lord / Jesus*) should not perish but have everlasting life" is just one among many. To sum up, as God called people in the Old Testament He does it in the New.

## Similarity of the church and Spiritual Israel

### A true Jew

Paul's teaching makes it clear that spiritual Israel has in many respects taken the place of literal Israel. "A man is not a Jew if he is only one outwardly, nor is circumcision merely outward and physical. No, a man is a Jew if he is one inwardly; and circumcision is circumcision of the heart, by the Spirit, not by the written code," (Romans 2: 28-29). To the Galatians he wrote: "If you belong to Christ, then you are Abraham's seed; and heirs according to the promise," (Romans 3:29).

### Promises

Furthermore, some of the promises directed to literal Israel in the Old Testament are regarded by New Testament writers as having been fulfilled in spiritual Israel, the church.[13] For example, Hosea wrote, "I will show my love to the one I called 'Not my loved one.' I will say to those called 'Not my people,' 'You are my people'; and they will say, 'You are my God,'" (Hosea 2:23). From Hosea 1:6-11 it is clear that this verse refers to Israel. Paul, however, applies it in Romans 9:24-25 to Jews and Gentiles alike.

A similar example, we find in the promise of Joel 2:28 about the outpouring of the Holy Spirit, fulfilled on the day of Pentecost in Acts 2:17.[14] By this example it should be noted, however, that Peter was speaking to and about Jews at this point (Acts 2:5, 22).

---

[13] Millard J. Erikson, *Christian Theology,* Second Edition (Grand Rapids, MI: Backer Academic, 2007), 1053.

[14] George E. Ladd, "Israel and the Church," *Evangelical Quarterly* 36, no. 4 (October-December 1964), 209.

## The presence of God

Another methapor of Pauls about the temple makes it clear that the Church has taken the place of literal Israel in many aspects. Both the Old Testament and Judaism anticipated the creation of a new temple in the Kingdom of God.[15] Ladd pointed out with regard to Matthew 16:18 that Jesus had spoken of the formation of His Church as the erection of a building. "I will destroy this temple that is made with hands, and in three days I will build another, not made with hands,"(Mark 14:58). Ladd concluded, that this was possibly understood by the early Christians to mean the establishment of the new messianic community.[16] While the primitive community continued as Jews to worship in the temple (Acts 2:46), Stephen was the first to realize that temple worship was irrelevant for Christians (Acts 7:48).[17] The place of Christian community took the place of the temple as the eschatological temple of God, as the place where God dwells and is worshipped. "The presence of God has removed from the Jerusalem temple to the new temple, the Christian church," as Gärnter states.[18]

## Faith not Law

"The Gentiles, who did not pursue righteousness, have attained to righteousness, even the righteousness of faith, but Israel, pursuing the law of righteousness, has not attained to the law of righteousness. Why? Because they did not seek it by faith, but as it were, by the works of the law. For they stumbled at that stumbling stone", (Romans 9:31-32). Jesus, the Messiah was the fulfilment of the law. After he fulfilled it, He abolished it, and we are now

---

[15]Ezekiel 37:26; Haggai 2:9

[16]George E. Ladd, *A theology of the New Testament*, (Grand Rapids, MI: Eerdmans, 1975), 540.

[17] Ibid.

[18] See B. Gärtner, The Temple and the Community in Quran and the NT (1965), 65; see also S. Hanson, The Unity of the Church in the NT (1964), 133.

under the new covenant and law of Christ (Ephesians 3:15 and Acts 15).[19] However, in Romans 10:2, Paul witnesses to Orthodox Jews that they have "a zeal for God" but "by seeking to establish their own righteousness, they have not submitted to the righteousness of God."

## Gentiles provoke Jews

In Romans 10:19, Paul quoted Moses "I will provoke you to jealousy by those who are not a nation, I will move you to anger by a foolish nation." By writing that he refers to the Gentiles who believe now, through faith in the Jewish Messiah. Expressing the living faith in the God of Abraham, Isaac and Jacob, the Church becomes a provocation to the Orthodox Jews.

## Difference between Israel and the Church

### Empirical Israel and Spiritual Israel

Paul clearly distinguishes between empirical Israel and spiritual Israel, between the people as a whole and the faithful remnant.[20] Romans 9:6 describe "For not all who are descended from Israel belong to Israel," (Romans 9:6). Here Paul sets over against Israel according to natural descent the true Israel who have been faithful to God.[21] While the nation as a whole has rejected her Messiah, there is a remnant chosen by grace who have believed (Romans 11:5).

---

[19] Larry Harriman, "Prophecy Made Simple – Israel and the Church – What is the Relationship between the two?" http://www.ifbreformation.org/Prophecy_Israel_Church.aspx (27 November 2007).

[20] George E. Ladd, *A theology of the New Testament*, 538.

[21] Ibid.

## The country of Israel

The predominant view was that the destruction of Israel and the temple by the Romans in 70 A.D. signalled the official and divinely-ordained end of the Jewish nation, never to be re-instituted as a national entity. The fact that Jerusalem laid in ruins, and the Jewish people were scattered over the world was seen as conclusive evidence that God was forever finished with national Israel.[22] But God's promise to restore the country[23] can be seen in the foundation of the new country Israel, in 1948, and his perpetuation in at least five existential wars.

Even though the Church has in many ways taken the place of Israel, we cannot say that the Church is Israel. This would be as ludicrous as claiming that "the land of Israel" is now "the land of the Church."[24]

## Spiritual Restoration

Israel is still the special people of God. Romans 11:15, promises that Israel will be saved. Yet Israel will be saved by entering the Church, just as the Gentiles. There is no statement anywhere in the New Testament that there is any other basis of salvation.[25]

Finally, the Church has to tell Judaism that they will never be able to understand what God has done for them in sending Jesus, unless in all humility they realize that it was their own fault that they lost the significance which by the will of God they should have throughout the history of mankind, and that their chance will not come merely by their waiting for it.[26]

---

[22] Thomas S. McCall, Israel and the Church, 3.

[23] Isaiah 11:10-12; Jeremiah 16:14-16; Ezekiel 36-37; Amos 9:14-15; Zachariah 8-14

[24] Dave Hunt, "Jews, Gentiles & the Church", http://www.menorah.org/jgc.html (26 November 2007), 3.

[25] Millard J. Erikson, *Christian Theology*, 1053.

[26] Otto A. Piper, „Church and Judaism in Holy History," *Theology Today* 18 (April 1961): 71.

# CONCLUSION

The writer of this paper disagrees with the replacement theology. He does not believe that Israel is just an appendix, a vestigial organ which is displaced by the Church. On the other hand, he does not agree with the dispensationalist view that Israel and the Church are two eternally separate entities which God deals with in different ways.

The paper showed like Ladd has noted, that the truth here, as in so many matters, lies somewhere between the two poles.[27] The Church has in many places taken the place of spiritual Israel; however there is a future for national Israel. The writer concludes that Israel will be saved by entering the church just as the Gentiles were (Romans 11:15).

---

[27] George E. Ladd, "Israel and the Church," *Evangelical Quarterly* 36, no. 4 (October-December 1964): 207.

## BIBLIOGRAPHY

Berkhof, Louis. *Systematic Theology.* Grand Rapids: Eerdmans, 1953.

Cairns, Earle. *Christianity Through the Centuries*, Michigan: Zondervan, 1996.

Chafer, Lewis. Systematic Theology, vol. 4. Dallas: Dallas Seminary, 1948.

Erikson, Millard. *Christian Theology*, Second Edition. Grand Rapids, MI: Backer Academic, 2007.

Erikson, Millard. *Introducing Christian Doctrine*. Grand Rapids, MI: Backer Academic, 2005.

Harriman, Larry. "Prophecy Made Simple – Israel and the Church – What is the Relationship between the two?" http://www.ifbreformation.org/Prophecy_Israel_Church.aspx (27 November 2007).

Hunt, Dave. "Jews, Gentiles & the Church." http://www.menorah.org/jgc.html (26 November 2007).

Ladd, George. "Israel and the Church." *Evangelical Quarterly* 36, no. 4 (October-December 1964).

Ladd, George. *A theology of the New Testament.* Grand Rapids, MI: Eerdmans, 1975.

McCall, Thomas. "What is the Olive Tree?" *in Levit Letter*, March 2001, http://www.levitt.com/essays/olivetree-church.html (24 November 2007).

McCall, Thomas. "Israel and the Church: the Differences", *in Levit Letter*, May 1996, http://www.levitt.com/essays/israel-church.html (24 November 2007).

Piper, Otto. "Church and Judaism in Holy History," *Theology Today* 18 (April 1961).

Sizer, Stephen. "An alternative theology of the Holy Land: a critique of Christian Zionism", *Churchman* (London) 113:125-46 no. 2 1999.

The New Thomsen Study Bible. Wollerau, CH: La Buona Novella Inc. Bible Publishing House, 2006.

CPSIA information can be obtained
at www.ICGtesting.com
Printed in the USA
BVHW050438110621
609157BV00008B/500

9 783656 223764